£14

THE WEDDING DRESS

THE WEDDING DRESS

A SOURCEBOOK

PHILIP DELAMORE

PAVILION

CONTENTS

INTRODUCTION 6

BALL GOWN 12

PRINCESS LINE 32

EMPIRE LINE 52

MERMAID AND FISHTAIL 68

A-LINE 92

COLUMN 108

MINI AND MIDI 120

THE SUIT 130

NECKLINES 140

BACKS 152

SLEEVES 164

VEILS 174

TRAINS 184

DETAILS 194

INDEX 220

DIRECTORY 221

ACKNOWLEDGEMENTS 222

INTRODUCTION

The wedding dress is such an evocative symbol of the bride. It has romantic and historical associations with the ritual of dress and the rites of ceremony, from countless princess brides encountered in fairytales as a child, to the televised and endlessly photographed weddings of royalty and celebrity that have punctuated our lives.

Today the wedding dress occupies a unique moment in your life. As ritual and ceremony is all but removed from our everyday experiences, the idea of wearing a special dress for only one day of your life imbues it with the significance of its symbolic heritage. While fashion may affect the silhouette, the white dress and veil have remained virtually unchanged in over 150 years.

The variety of styles, details and fabric combinations available to today's bride may however seem a little bewildering. If you do not know an A-Line from a princess line, or a sweetheart neckline from a picture collar then read on.

This book is intended as a sourcebook for you, as a helpful guide for inspiration, ideas and visual reference, not only to help with your choice of wedding dress, but also to help communicate it to others. That picture/thousand-word analogy is never more true than when trying to communicate the abstract ideas of design, and the emotions of romance to others. Use this book, along with other reference material you gather from the bridal stores and magazines to build a picture, both of yourself and your dress, to help all the other people involved in the process, from the shop assistant to the

"I chose my wife, as she did her wedding gown,
for qualities that would wear well."

OLIVER GOLDSMITH, c.1760

caterer, who will need to have a good idea of your vision. Even if you don't feel like you have much vision yet, this book should help in the process of developing one.

You will need to know three things:

KNOW YOURSELF

Unless you are Jennifer Lopez, who, let's face it, must know what kind of dress suits her best by now, you need to start with a little self-analysis. If you have never done anything traditional in your life it is not the time to start just because you feel it is expected. The diversity of wedding experiences available now are limited only by your imagination, but if you have lived a life of expectation that you would sweep down the aisle in a fairytale ball gown, then don't compromise.

You might want to think about what your favourite dress is, and if you don't have one you might like to consider that there are other options, such as a suit or more casual two piece outfits. Do you have a personality that you tend to express by the way you dress, or do you dress to blend in. Trying a few dresses at a bridal store or boutique with an honest friend can also be a good start to see what does and doesn't suit you, especially if you are not used to dressing up (*listen* to the honest friend). Try on a range of styles and colours, and use the experience of the staff to help you make some initial decisions about what you look and feel comfortable in. Once you have an idea of what works for you then you can be more confident about choosing.

KNOW YOUR BUDGET

The dress is one of the biggest purchases for a wedding, so you need to budget for this whether you are buying a simple suit or dress off the peg, or having a couture dress made for you. Like house buying this can tend to go out of the window when you see something you like, but remember that if you are having a dress made for you there is lots of flexibility, and you can discuss how to get what you want for the budget you have. The idea of couture being the expensive option is not necessarily true.

Remember not to rush into ordering, and look at the options available to you – not only at the department stores and specialist bridal stores, but also vintage

*"A dress should never overpower the wearer. It should merely
be an appropriate frame for a charming picture, bringing out
the beauties of the picture, but never distracting attention
from it. So few women understand this."*

CHARLES WORTH, *HARPER'S BAZAAR* PERSONAL COLUMN, DECEMBER 15, 1877

and antiquarian clothing stores, costume and period hire specialists and individual dressmakers. Ask friends for personal recommendations and make use of the internet to view designers' collections or even bid for a vintage piece.

KNOW YOUR LIMITATIONS

I don't mean you shouldn't do anything unexpected, but rather consider all those external factors which you may have no control over. For example, are there any religious restrictions on what you may not, or may have to wear for the ceremony (Jewish weddings require a veil for example). Will your cathedral train fit in the motorbike sidecar you are arriving at the church in? If you are getting married abroad, on a beach in Hawaii, there may be simple practical issues of transporting your dress, or perhaps that white bikini is a better option.

USING THIS BOOK

While I have included a brief historical resume of each style, along with suggestions for whom the style may be better suited to and classic examples of the style and fabrics used, this is by no means an historical work on the wedding dress, and should not be taken as such. Many of the styles fall into several categories and it is arguable as to where to draw the boundaries between them. Some styles belong to specific periods in time, while others refer to specific constructions or cuts.

Don't be fazed by the almost overwhelming choice there appears to be out there. At the start of the 21st century you simply need to remember that a lot of weddings

"Talk six times with the same single lady and
you may get the wedding dress ready."
LORD BYRON

Married in white, you have chosen right,

Married in green, ashamed to be seen,

Married in grey, you'll go far away,

Married in red, you'll wish yourself dead,

Married in blue, you'll always be true,

Married in yellow, ashamed of your fellow,

Married in black, you'll wish yourself back,

Married in pink, of you he will think.

OLD ENGLISH RHYME

have preceded yours. As each bride has expressed herself through personal, religious and fashionable desires, so a myriad of styles and combinations of dress have evolved.

Each of the chapters of this book will guide you through the basic silhouettes, some enduring classics, some fashion *faux pas*, and some of the details you will want to consider when embellishing upon that silhouette.

Finally, perhaps it is worth remembering the words of the ancient rhyme above, when planning your colour scheme.

BALL GOWN

BALL GOWN

STYLE

As the enduring image of the archetypal wedding dress, the ball gown epitomises the romantic idea of the fairytale princess bride. The fitted bodice and voluminous skirts, petticoats, train and veil in diaphanous layers seems to be the definitive bridal statement. Ball gowns have fitted bodices and full skirts. They tend to be one piece, but may comprise of top and separate skirts. The skirts usually skim the floor, with petticoats or hoops resembling the original Victorian crinolines to give the required fullness. The distribution of this fullness can vary – so consider whether you want a ballerina style with circular skirts, or whether a bustled style with fullness at the back which allows you to keep a flatter front profile is better suited.

Bodices come in many variants from strapless basque or corseted types, with straps or sleeves, to off-the-shoulder picture collars and fully fitted high necks.

HISTORY

It is interesting to consider that the elements of shape and colour which define the classic white wedding dress did not really come together until the middle of the nineteenth century with the wedding of Queen Victoria and Albert. Perhaps it is the romance of a royal wedding, that was for love, rather than in the tradition of political and financial convenience, where the bride and groom would have rarely met prior to the ceremony, which has endured.

The Victorian era was pivotal in the development of fashion as an industry, where the dressmaker turned into the designer. The invention of the domestic sewing machine, the industrialisation of textile production for fabrics such as lace, and the establishment of the first couture houses in Paris during the reign of Victoria, created a consumer market for fashion to an aspirational *nouveau riche*, and a burgeoning middle class. Journalism and an opening up of international markets, particularly in the New World, saw illustrated journals describe in detail every aspect of the court seasons and events including numerous fashion plates and patterns, which could be recreated by the home dressmaker if a couturier was beyond your means.

It is easy to forget that this style of dress was actually not far from the normal everyday dress of the period, and dresses were often altered to be worn again for other formal occasions. Queen Victoria herself set the example by frequently using the lace overskirt from her wedding dress – wearing it over black silk for her Diamond Jubilee celebrations over 50 years later.

Today it is more rare that the bride considers wearing her dress for another occasion, unless perhaps it is a more contemporary style of dress or suit.

CLASSICS
As it is a perennial favourite you will have plenty of choice in this style. The precedent has been set in a century of royal weddings, both real and on screen. Think of Liz Taylor (first time around) and Grace Kelly as the ultimate Hollywood royalty-turned-princess bride, and none more evocative and overblown than Diana Spencer's fairytale Emanuel creation (see page 17). More recently celebrities have returned to this style statement, including Mariah Carey and, of course, Victoria Beckham.

More casual modern variants on this style include the 1950's-style quilted skirt and cardigan, and simple crossover wrapped blouse worn over a full skirt.

WHO SHOULD WEAR
Strapless is great if you are of tall slim build, and tend to be broad shouldered. If you have the height but are narrow on top, or feel uncomfortable exposing so much, then opt for a more covered up version with straps or sleeves and a high neck. This style can still work if you are medium height or tend towards pear shaped, as you can emphasise the waist and disguise broader hips with a full skirt. The corseted style can also work for a fuller bust by placing emphasis at the waist. Higher shoes and hair worn up can help emphasise a lean silhouette. Remember long opera gloves can look great with a strapless gown, adding drama while reducing the amount of exposure, especially if you are unsure about baring your arms.

If you are planning on having a train, then the ballgown is the style of dress to do it with. Consider whether you want the train to be attached or detachable, and how grand a statement you want to make with it (see Trains on pages 186-7).

FABRICS
Lots of options here, and often the bodice and skirts will have variations. Satins and taffetas, with lace overlaid or as trimming, are a classic look. Be aware that silks like this will always crease, especially the more papery silks like dupion which should be avoided. If you want something that looks clean and unwrinkled there are some good synthetic alternatives available now. The skirts may have many layers of tulle petticoats to give volume to the skirts, or indeed may compromise the whole skirt, encased in sheer swathes of chiffon or voile in the more 1950's style gowns. The bodice may be of a contrasting fabric to the skirt, or have elaborate beading, appliqué or embroidery which cascades from the bodice and scatters across the skirt.

LEFT Elizabeth Taylor weds Nicky
Hilton in 1950 in a white satin dress by
MGM studio designer Helen Rose.

ABOVE AND RIGHT Grace Kelly wears
a Helen Rose dress in a renaissance
style, with a bell shaped skirt and rose
point lace bodice, for her wedding to
Prince Rainier of Monaco, 1956.

BELOW Lady Diana's iconic Emanuel
gown for her wedding to Prince
Charles in 1981.

ABOVE Phillipa Lepley's strapless silk zibeline design is cinched at the waist with a silk rose and feather corsage and features a delicate hand beaded trim.

RIGHT Flowers make a bold statement in this full skirted design with a corsage at the hip trimming a long fluid train, and balanced by a beautiful hairpiece.

ABOVE, CLOCKWISE FROM TOP LEFT Cobweb lace with crystal dewdrops on a silver base; clusters of beads in a two layered bodice divide the body at the widest and narrowest points; scalloped edges trimmed with beads and wrap over effect add interest while narrowing the silhouette; spaghetti straps and cascading embroidery draw the eye across and down the dress. OPPOSITE This sweetheart neckline is softened with floral appliqués to the bodice which scatter onto the skirt of this prom style dress.

TOP RIGHT The swathed bodice of this dress is echoed by the swept back skirt into a bustled train. Diamante straps appear to fall from the shoulders.

BELOW RIGHT *Fin de siècle* – this dress by Elizabeth Todd combines a provocative low-cut corset bodice with the soft clouds of a multi-layered tulle skirt.

OPPOSITE Another daring corset top with winged sides and asymmetrical embellishment, unfolds into a bell shaped satin skirt.

LEFT Innocent looks – lace inserted to the point of this basque bodiced dress is simple and pretty. ABOVE, CLOCKWISE FROM TOP LEFT Asymmetric details in these dresses create focal points. A cascade of fabric swathes soften the silhouette; a simple strapless dress gathered at the hip with a silk corsage; a tearose dress with lace overlay and pleated skirt; a white coatdress over a strapless foundation gives contrast in texture and tone.

OPPOSITE The simple column dress in the background is upstaged by the voluminous tulle skirts of the dress being photographed by Hardy Amies – both are his own wedding dress designs, 1960.

ABOVE Two more modern examples of tulle ball gown skirts, showing the striking emphasis to the waist (top), and a soft matching veil (bottom).

LEFT The "Godiva" dress — a strapless Italian floral print gown with silk organza overlay, designed by Phillipa Lepley. It features a "cupped" bustier bodice and a flat-fronted full skirt.

BELOW Daring coloured highlights make this low-cut dress stand out from the crowd. A sheer green overskirt is scattered with silk hydrangeas in gold, lilac and blue.

RIGHT Subtle combinations of colour complement different skin tones. This SaraSusa ivory and cream satin dress with rose details is good for fair skin.

BELOW RIGHT "Married in blue, he will always be true" — this colour looks good on olive and darker skin tones.

BELOW FAR RIGHT A rose tint on the bows and cross-over bodice and train of this SaraSusa dress complements pinker tones.

OPPOSITE A seamed bodice is echoed in the pleats of the bell skirt in this subtle gold gown.

BELOW An ivory strapless dress with large pleated bell shaped skirt is striking in its classic simplicity.

PRINCESS LINE

PRINCESS LINE

STYLE

A very flattering and useful style, the princess line is not so much a silhouette as a cut. It tends to be closely associated with the fit and flare of the A-line, but for the purpose of establishing the different dress styles within this guide, the princess line flows unbroken from top to bottom, dividing the dress into vertical panels, while an A-line style may have horizontal seams to define the waist. The princess line is characterized by vertical style lines from the shoulder or curving from the armhole to the hem of the dress. These incorporate the fit, and shape the dress so no other darts or pleats are necessary. Consequently the style is clean, minimal, and most importantly slimming. Not only used for dresses, you will also find the princess line used for jackets and coats, and it is a favourite cut for women's tailoring.

Ultra-versatile, the princess line can be used to create a number of definitive styles from mini and shift dresses, elegant sheaths and columns, to bell skirts, circular hems and fishtails. It is also a cut often used to create bridal coats and coatdresses, like the one worn by Sophie of Wessex at her wedding to Prince Edward (see page 72).

HISTORY

The princess line is generally attributed to Charles Worth, the nineteenth century couturier who created the wedding dress for Princess Alexandra for her marriage to Edward VII. Worth was an English designer who established the first couture house in Paris in 1858, and was responsible for many innovative styles adopted during the latter nineteenth and early twentieth century.

The princess line was named after Princess Alexandra and was developed from a desire to eliminate the need for separate bodice and skirt in the construction of the dress. It set a standard that has been universally adopted, and is a perennial favourite with designers such as Yves Saint Laurent and Marc Jacobs.

In combination with an A-line silhouette, this cut was definitive of the 1960's styles from designers like Courrèges, Cardin and Mary Quant (see also A-line, pages 92–107) who used the cut to create clean space-aged designs. Again in the 1980s designers like Jean Paul Gaultier used the contouring effects of the style with corsetry fabrics to create sexy curves on celebrity clients like Madonna.

CLASSICS

As I have already described the versatility of the princess line, once you start to look for it you will see it everywhere. The classic example is a fit and flare silhouette which may be strapless or with sleeves like the one worn by Queen Elizabeth II. As Princess Elizabeth she wore a Norman Hartnell satin dress with lace décolletage in this style for her wedding to Prince Philip in 1947 (see page 36). Half a century later Lady Helen Windsor chose a modern take in Catherine Walker's dress of the same style.

If you are considering a winter wedding then a high neck long sleeved princess line coatdress with hat and muff is a great look. This style can also look stunning in lace and all-over textures where the silhouette remains uncluttered and elegant. Ivory or metallic laces over subtle base colours can work well, and how about black lace over cream if you want to turn heads. Embellishments tend to be placed at the neck or hem, so as not to interfere with the clean lines, but a cascading motif can add interest, and a bold print can give it wow factor (see page 50).

WHO SHOULD WEAR

Ideal for creating a statement that is sculptural and uncluttered, the strong verticals add height and reduce the visual impact of a large expanse of uninterrupted fabric. With so many possibilities on offer, this style will suit most body types and heights. Particularly good on tall curvaceous figures, this cut can also give the illusion of curves where they are in fact wishful thinking. Teamed with the right underwear the shaping effect at the waist and fulness of the skirt can also disguise wide hips and bums. In shift and shorter incarnations it is ideal for petite and boyish, straight up and down figures. If you have a long body and relatively short legs, the high waist and shape and flare of the skirt can help re-proportion you. There are lots of neckline and collar options which work well with the princess line. If it is cut straight from the shoulder seam, then it works well with a high neck style; while the curved princess line from the armhole complements round, bateau and scoop necks (see also Necklines on pages 142-143).

FABRICS

Sculptural shapes tend to benefit from unfussy fabrics, and the classic princess line would be in duchesse satin, peau de soie, or similar fabrics that have weight and structure, while the skirts can be given extra volume with petticoats. If you are going for a bolder statement like the textured, lace or two layer constructions then you might consider damasks.

ABOVE Carmen Electra in an ivory Badgley Mischka dress, 2003.

RIGHT Roses clustered along a sweetheart neckline add interest to the classic simplicity of this SaraSusa designed gown. This is a replica of the style chosen by *Little House on the Prairie* star, Melissa Gilbert.

OPPOSITE Royal Princess, Elizabeth II wears Norman Hartnell for her wedding to Prince Philip in 1947. The dress was inspired by Botticelli's *Primavera*, and the white satin dress was embellished with seed pearls and ten thousand crystals in the form of white York roses, orange blossom, lilacs, jasmine and wheat.

RIGHT A dramatic entrance in a square neck princess line dress with symmetrical embroidery on the bodice and stylish opera length gloves.

ABOVE LEFT Utterly simple, this dress relies on classic structural impact and is adorned with just a little decorative beading along the strapless neckline.

BELOW LEFT This Caroline Parkes design in silver lace needs no other detail to make a statement.

OPPOSITE Layers of silk ruffles on this stunning Caroline Castigliano Collection dress add textural interest while the line of the gown remains unbroken.

OPPOSITE The embroidered details on this silver dress follow the princess line contours of the gown culminating in decorative straps

RIGHT Delicate embroidered floral motifs cascade down a white satin dress.

LEFT This Caroline Parkes gown has lace overlaid on satin, with a straight-through cut finishing in a small train. A simple, fluid design.

RIGHT Coloured lace and beaded appliqué create a very different effect with asymmetric detailing on this full-skirted dress.

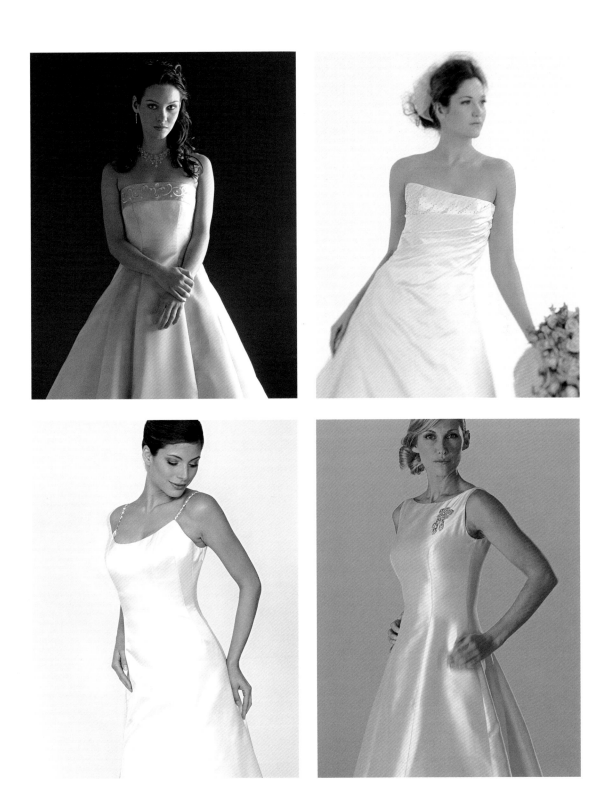

LEFT Spaghetti straps suspend a white satin dress sprinkled with crystal beads,
which echo the diamanté headband.

ABOVE, CLOCKWISE FROM TOP LEFT Embroidered border trim adds interest to this uncluttered design;
an asymmetrically draped bodice is subtly sprinkled with beads; a brooch sparkles on a simple gold
Stewart Parvin design; jewelled straps set off the clean lines of this white dress by Caroline Parkes.

PRINCESS LINE

OPPOSITE A striking floral headpiece is echoed in the embroidery of this draped and full skirted gold dress.

ABOVE RIGHT Wing fronted bodice with beads on a dress with trumpet style train.

BELOW RIGHT This gown features an inverted "V" detail on the bodice and a deep inverted pleat skirt.

BELOW A Caroline Parkes strapless design with bold rose print – a dress that begs to be noticed.
OPPOSITE This pretty off-the-shoulder gown features a gathered bodice and
radial beaded details.

EMPIRE LINE

EMPIRE LINE

STYLE

The empire line is defined by a raised waistline cut just beneath the bust, often gathering a full dress, which drops to the floor to give an elongated silhouette. The neckline is traditionally a deep square décolletage which is either worn with straps cut wide on the shoulder, or with capped or long sleeves. Dresses often feature a short round train at the back, as the fabric falls smoothly from the high waist to the floor, sometimes over a small pad similar to the bustle, which separates the dress from the body. Historically this style of dress was often worn with a cropped bolero or Spencer Jacket in velvet or brocade, or with a Pelerine (a shaped wrap). Alternatively a long matching coat called a Pelisse could be worn over the dress. This has the same high waistline, at which it is fastened, falling open to the floor to reveal the dress beneath.

More contemporary takes on the empire line include strapless versions, and free-flowing A-line and mermaid skirts. A variation on the empire is the trapeze-line, which is not waisted, but flares directly from the underarm to hem.

The empire style is often embellished with embroidery, lace appliqué or beading to the bodice (see Kate Winslet's fine example on page 56). The emphasis of the raised waistline is also often highlighted with ribbon, bows or contrasting fabric to the skirt of the dress.

HISTORY

This style became fashionable during the Regency period (1790–1825) where it originated in France. It was inspired by the Greco-Roman style of draped tunic worn by classical figures which became popular as the Napoleonic Empire spread across Europe into the Middle East. The fashion, which was relatively short-lived, symbolized a period of classical enlightenment and unrestrained dressing for women, and it was epitomized by the heroines of Jane Austen's novels, such as Catherine Morland in *Northanger Abbey*. Subsequently the heavily constructed and corseted clothing which became fashionable throughout the remainder of the nineteenth century actually encumbered women.

Its short-lived popularity may have been due to the French influenza epidemic which swept England during this time and was branded the "muslin disease" after the flimsy style, which was at odds with the often inclement English weather. Added to this was the fashion for the empire style dress to cling to the curves of the body, and it is recorded that women would actually dampen their petticoats to allow the fabric of the dress to do this.

Revived at the beginning of the twentieth century by the French couturier Paul Poiret, the style had much in common with the dress reform of the period, and many designers were influenced by this classical silhouette. It has subsequently remained a popular style throughout the last century – in the early 1970's revival for Deco with designers such as Barbara Hulanicki for Biba, and in the late 1980's with John Galliano and Romeo Gigli. It is perhaps testament to the romantic associations with the many film and television adaptations of Jane Austen's novels that the style has recently become popular for wedding dresses once again.

CLASSICS

Classics can range from an authentic recreation of the period style, perched on a *chaise longue* with an ostrich feather fan, to Audrey Hepburn as Holly Golightly in *My Fair Lady* in a sparkling Hollywood version of the empire line, gathered at the bust with sheer beaded capped sleeves and opera length white gloves. You can choose from a number of interpretations from the decades described to pick the perfect incarnation for you.

WHO SHOULD WEAR

The empire style is a good all-rounder, suitable for most physiques, as illustrated in the following pages: famous actresses Kate Winslet, Liv Tyler and Emily Mortimer (pages 56-7) show the versatility of the style for flattering different body shapes and sizes. The high waist elongates the body and hides lumps and bumps. It is ideal for those with a small bust, short legs or a long body and the pear shaped figure. It can also help minimize a large bust if cut correctly, and it makes a natural maternity style.

FABRICS

The style is traditionally made from light cotton fabrics such as muslin and lawn, with details in Broderie Anglais or embroidery of classical motifs. It works equally well in sheer silk chiffon, georgette or voile laid over a base fabric. Colour variations in pale shades and metallics, and with delicate beaded embellishment can update the look.

LEFT Kate Winslet marries Jim Threapleton in a stunning white beaded dress by designer Alexander McQueen, 1998.

ABOVE RIGHT Actress Emily Mortimer's delicate pale yellow empire line dress was a vintage find in London antique emporium Virginia. It featured traditional sheer capped sleeves and a front buttoning detail.

BELOW RIGHT Liv Tyler weds in a simple, ethereal empire line dress by Alexander McQueen, with draped sleeves and a deep scoop décolletage. A band of gold brocade adds interest and her shoes match the groom's tie.

BELOW A pretty damask train trimmed with daisy border, hem and headband in this vintage empire line dress.

OPPOSITE Full-length trapeze style dress by Jeanne Lanvin in ribbed voile with high waisted sash and matching wide brimmed floppy hat, 1968.

ABOVE Latticework appliqué adorns the bodice of this cap-sleeved dress with split sheer skirt overlay.

OPPOSITE Sheer simplicity, a chapel length veil and pearls set off this elegant dress with spaghetti straps and lace appliqué detail.

OPPOSITE Crystal beaded and silver embroidered sheer skirt over a strapless empire line dress with chapel train, set off by a sparkly choker.

BELOW Lace-trimmed petticoats are pretty under organza ruffles on the hem and bustier of this off-the-shoulder Caroline Parkes gown.

LEFT Pre-Raphaelite looks in a simple low cut dress with crystal spaghetti straps.

OPPOSITE Romantic and sophisticated, an ivory dress with pearl details and embroidered overskirt which flows into a train.

FOLLOWING PAGE, LEFT "Elliot" – a Phillipa Lepley design in duchess satin, with a crepe and chiffon bias cut skirt and a flower and streamer ribbon corsage to adorn the bust.

FOLLOWING PAGE, RIGHT Modern elegance in a fluid bias cut crepe dress with empire line and pin-tuck chiffon sleeves by designer Sarah Owen.

MERMAID
AND FISHTAIL

MERMAID AND FISHTAIL

STYLE

The mermaid or fishtail dress is usually associated with a bias-cut style typical of the 1930's Hollywood siren, a quicksilver sheath which seems to collect in a pool as it hits the floor. A fluid alternative to the constructed column style (see also Column on pages 108-9), it is a sheath which fits where it touches the body. The fabric is cut diagonally to the grain, allowing it to drape around the body so that dresses often require no fastenings or openings and can be slipped over the head, much as if you were wearing a knitted jersey or stretch lycra dress (which is of course an option, but only for the physically and emotionally confident!).

Most dresses in the bias-style tend not to actually be cut on the bias, but give the same visual effect, as bias cutting involves quite a lot of diagonal seaming within the construction. True bias-cut dresses of the 1930's period tended to have circular hems in trumpet or fishtail shapes.

The mermaid dress is typically figure-hugging to the knee, then flares to the hem. This can be achieved in a number of different ways, by adding godets (triangular inserts) to give fullness, or by adding volume evenly through the vertical panels of a princess line. Alternatively a circular panel can seam horizontally at or above the knee to add a lot of volume. The distribution of the "fishtail" can vary dramatically, it can be a trumpet or circular hem, a hem that is only apparent from the back, as a train, or even gathered to the front in a flamenco style.

HISTORY

Madeleine Vionnet was a pioneer of bias-cutting in the 1920's and 1930's, and like Fortuny's pleated columns, the fluid cling and drape of fabric cut in this way was evocative of classical Greek dress. The style was immortalised by Hoyningen-Huene in a photograph of a Vionnet dress as a "bas-relief" for *Vogue* in 1931, reminiscent of the Elgin marbles. Vionnet was, and still is, revered as an extraordinary talent whose designs transcend her era, with Dior, Alaia, Galliano and Miyake all citing her influence on their work. Actresses of the period such as Marlene Dietrich, Joan Crawford and Katherine Hepburn wore Vionnet both on and off screen. This was also the time when the influence of Hollywood really began to challenge Parisian couturiers as the arbiters of taste, with designers such as Adrian of Hollywood establishing retail business from dressing many of the stars of the silver screen. This relationship with the media still endures, and can be seen on the red carpet at the Oscars, as well as the film and television successes that influence what we wear today.

The slip dress, rather than a true bias cut dress, can be traced back further. As an item of underwear a silk slip was favoured with the early nineteenth century empire styles, but has only more recently become an item of outerwear. Since the 1970's the slip has evolved to become one of the most popular styles of dress, particularly with US designers like Calvin Klein and Betsey Johnson.

CLASSICS

The style is typified by the slim sheath dress to the knee with a draped or cowl neck and flowing trailing skirt. Think of Jean Harlow or Mae West and 1930's Hollywood, with a figure hugging dress and circular cut fishtail inserted asymmetrically at the knee. A contemporary take on the Vionnet classic bias dress for brides can be found at Catherine Walker, who has dressed many famous brides and celebrities.

The coatdress worn by Sophie Wessex in her wedding to Prince Edward shows a good example of the classic mermaid skirt, cut flat to the front with volume at the back allowing the skirts to flow in a train behind her (see page 72). American film actress Denise Richards wears a slip dress for her wedding to Charlie Sheen, for a more relaxed and modern take on the style (see page 73).

WHO SHOULD WEAR

You don't have to be tall to wear bias cut, but you need to be slim or athletic to carry it off. The rule goes that if you are not confident about wearing a bias dress without underwear, then perhaps you shouldn't wear one. Unsightly straps and fittings can mar the cling of the dress. If you are really skinny or very flat chested you may be better advised to go for a slip dress or a more constructed style, which will also suit tall curvaceous shapes, as the volume at the hem can balance hips and bust.

FABRICS

The mermaid skirt will work with many of the other styles already covered in this guide, particularly the princess and column style of dress, and it works equally well in stiff constructed fabrics. Contrasting fabrics can work well too, for example velvet, inset with a contrasting fabric for the fishtail gives textural interest. Other silks such as crepe, georgette, mousseline, organza and gazar work well for this type of dress. Slip dress styles tend to be in satin, crepe de chine and lace, or for something more dramatic in fringed, beaded or sequinned fabrics.

ABOVE Sophie Rhys-Jones marries Prince Edward at St. Georges Chapel,
Windsor, in a fishtail coatdress designed by Samantha Shaw, 1999.
OPPOSITE TOP Actress Anne Heche poses with her new husband in a scoop
neck dress with capped sleeves, 2001.

BELOW RIGHT Denise Richards wears
an antique white slip dress by designer
Georgio Armani for her wedding to
Charlie Sheen, 2002.

ABOVE LEFT This shaped ivory zibeline silk sheath dress with puddle train creates the classic structured mermaid silhouette. It is set off with the addition of a rabbit fur bolero jacket.

BELOW LEFT On the lawn, the bride wears an empire line fluid mermaid dress by Antonia Pugh-Thomas with pearl beaded neck and armhole trim.

OPPOSITE Spiral cut dress with square neck, silver beaded floral motifs and edge trim.

OPPOSITE Chainmail – striking silver satin dress with silver crochet knit top trimmed with lace and crystal.

RIGHT Sheer simplicity – this apparently seamless sheath has a soft chiffon layer over satin. The perfect backdrop for some statement accessories.

OPPOSITE Antique white bias cut mermaid dress with spiral appliqué cut lace and halterneck.
BELOW LEFT White strapless dress with lace sheathed bodice.
BELOW RIGHT A Stewart Parvin design in cream crepe satin with empire waist and cowl neckline.

LEFT A deep V-neck scattered with crystal beading adorns a figure-hugging fishtail dress.

RIGHT The classic, understated, flowing lines of this mermaid dress with draped cowl neck and sheer bell-shaped sleeves, are injected with a touch of humour with the addition of this striking Cozmo Jenks headpiece.

OPPOSITE Rites of Spring – a simple
bias cut gown with halterneck and an
all over embroidered spiral design.

ABOVE RIGHT Champagne structured
bodice with lace appliqué over a satin
base. The appliqué continues down the
two-tiered skirt which is hemmed
with a scalloped edge.

BELOW RIGHT This simple bodice
is cut in many shaped panels and is
decorated with a symmetrical motif
which complements the accessories.

LEFT Antique style buttermilk lace slip over a soft blue-grey bias cut dress with spaghetti straps by Stewart Parvin.

OPPOSITE A beautiful bias spotted chiffon dress with circular hem and tiered skirts contrasts with the lace covered basque which encases the body.

RIGHT Back views – a deep V in
the back of this ivory duchess satin
column gown with covered buttons
draws a line to the large trailing fishtail
skirt. The bridesmaids wear narrower-
cut mermaid skirts.

MERMAID AND FISHTAIL

LEFT Irridescent beads flash
on the ruffled flamenco skirts
of this Yumi Katsura dress
modelled at a wedding fashion
show in Beijing, 2005.

OPPOSITE Pleats in the sheer back
of this boat-necked dress are at
once revealing and dramatic,
adding strong verticals to the
cathedral length train.

LEFT A vintage beaded 1920's dress is cleverly spliced with an ivory crushed velvet mermaid skirt and chiffon sleeves in this dress designed by the bride, Patrizia Hopkins, and made by Gussam at Fredek.

OPPOSITE This luxurious silk duchess satin column dress, designed by Sarah Owen, features a fishtail panel of sunray pleated organza which gives the dress a lighter feel. The bodice is hand-embroidered with pearl beads, encrusted with crystals .

A-LINE

A-LINE

STYLE

As the name suggests, the A-line has a fitted bodice and flared skirt. It is a pared down and more modern take on the classic ball gown shape, and is probably the most popular style of wedding dress seen today. We define the A-line as having a horizontal seam at the waist, and it can appear either sculptural and clean in fabrics that support the shape, or soft and flowing in lighter weights. The bodice and skirt flow together harmoniously in the A-line, but may still be in contrasting fabrics or textures, and the line is rather straighter than the curving crown of a skirt in the ball gown style. A-line skirts can still be full and circular or have pleats to give added volume, but more commonly the skirt will flare gently from waist to hem. Lengths can be anything from daring mini to elegant floor sweeping skirts with trains.

HISTORY

The A-line is essentially a child of the 1960s, but we can see it emerge as a reaction to the utility dressing and boxy, mannish style imposed by the Second World War. Dior's 1947 Corolla collection which introduced the "New Look", a strongly feminine style with a cinched waist, padded hips and full skirt, set off the trend, and Dior is credited with the origination of the notation for this style, as each of his lines was identified by a letter, this one being the letter "A". His protégé Yves Saint Laurent developed the silhouette throughout the 1950s and 1960s for his own label, as well as Givenchy, Courrèges and Emanuel Ungaro, who all trained at the house of Balenciaga, and were instrumental in the popularity of the A-Line silhouette throughout the 1960s, often teaming it with more experimental space-age materials. The A-line was also the shape of the mini and maxi dress styles popular at the end of the 1960s (see Mini and Midi, pages 120–129). By the 1970s it was reinvented in more natural fabrics, and the silhouette softened with designers like Ossie Clarke and Jean Muir giving it a new, less structural direction in jerseys and flowing sheers. Like the princess line, which is often the partner to the A-line silhouette, it is now a staple of any designer's collection, as popular now as it was 50 years ago.

CLASSICS

A strapless A-line dress that sweeps to the floor is currently one of the most popular requests for a wedding dress, more popular now than the traditional ball gown style, and a number of variations on this theme can be seen on the following pages. The bodice may be seamed into the skirt of the dress to give a clean silhouette, or in a contrasting fabric, texture or lace overlay for example to separate top from skirt visually. Balmain's 1954 wedding dress for Audrey Hepburn shows a shorter cocktail style of dress, the bound waist and full skirt reminiscent of the "New Look" style, and while the high neck and long sleeves are modest, the semi-sheer fabric hints at more. The shorter calf length skirt of the "prom" style dress has also become very fashionable once again with the red carpet set and these more 50's style dresses offer a pretty yet practical style for a civil ceremony. Softer A-Line silhouettes tend to be quite covered-up styles with sleeves (see page 101).

WHO SHOULD WEAR

This style is pretty universal, and one of the incarnations is sure to suit; it will just depend on how the dress is proportioned to your body shape. Like the empire line this style is elongating on a petite frame, and the waist emphasis can help define a shapely figure. Tiered layers of lace on Jennifer Lopez's wedding dress by Valentino (see page 96) show how the silhouette flatters and camouflages a pear shaped body, while halter and deep scoops or picture collars can emphasize the Dioresque. If you have great legs then the hemline can rise as far as a minidress for the daring, or drop to the floor in a train for the more traditional. Remember you can add height with heels under floor length dresses, but beware of heel fatigue by the end of the day if you are not used to wearing them.

FABRICS

If you are emphasizing the simplicity of the style then more structural silks like duchesse satin, grosgrain, shantung or damasks work well. Strapless styles may use contrast on the bodice, either in lace or beaded and embroidered details, or with a matte fabric which contrasts with a lustrous skirt. Sheer organza and laces layered over supporting base fabrics work well, and softer layers of voile, chiffon and even silk, viscose and wool jerseys are options for a more fluid or draped silhouette.

ABOVE LEFT Audrey Hepburn and Mel Ferrer leave the chapel after their wedding at Burgenstock Mountain, 1957. She wears a Balmain dress with sheer sleeves and cocktail length skirt.

BELOW LEFT AND OPPOSITE Jennifer Lopez wears Valentino for her wedding in 2001. The delicate Chantilly lace and silk dress with plunging neckline falls in tiers with scalloped hem and matching veil. The original Valentino illustration is shown opposite.

OPPOSITE A simple belt with diamanté buckle adds the finishing touch to this strapless ivory Caroline Parkes design. ABOVE, CLOCKWISE FROM TOP LEFT Variations on a theme with these strapless A-line dresses. Wing sided corset bodice and skirt in silver silk sari fabric with paisley motif; ivory damask bodice with plain wrap skirt and pleated sash; deep pleated bodice with beaded border in duchesse satin; broderie anglais boat neck overlay top, cut in a princess line.

ABOVE LEFT Emily Morrison and
Beth Milsom of Special Occasions
designed this dress with an
asymmetric overlaid sheath of
embroidered metallic organza.

ABOVE RIGHT A softer silhouette
in this 1960's vintage dress with
puffed shoulders and covered buttons
at the front.

BELOW RIGHT Asymmetrical details on
a white silk gown with organza silk
flowers decorating a single strap.

OPPOSITE Belle of the ball in striking
peacock feather embroidered gown
and stretch satin gloves.

A-LINE

OPPOSITE Antique white full skirts under a beaded and embroidered strapless bodice.

ABOVE RIGHT Godets add fullness to the skirt of this square necked dress with appliqué and beading which cascade from the bodice.

CENTRE RIGHT The classic A-line silhouette of this dress has an interesting bib-bodice with crumb-catcher neckline, and a pretty satin edged veil finishes the look.

BELOW RIGHT Petticoats hold the bell shape of this *Dangerous Liasons*-style dress with beaded bust-skimming bodice.

ABOVE Lace is overlaid on the bodice of this slip dress with cascading net veil and floral wreath.

OPPOSITE A simple white satin strapless dress with horizontal bands and beaded trim.

TOP LEFT Spiral cut dress with silver beaded floral motifs.

TOP RIGHT A wide satin band emphasizes the shoulders in this Caroline Parkes dress with sequinned bodice.

CENTRE LEFT Soft chiffon draped corset bodice in a magnolia silk crepe dress by Antonia Pugh-Thomas.

CENTRE RIGHT Pleated chiffon V-necked goddess dress by Caroline Parkes.

BOTTOM LEFT Bands of beading add texture to this wide scoop neck bodice with A-line skirt.

BOTTOM RIGHT Cleverly wrapped and pleated asymmetric dress with a beaded border on an ivory strapless gown.

OPPOSITE Silk zibeline A-line dress with asymmetrical embroidery and beading by designer Sarah Owen.

COLUMN

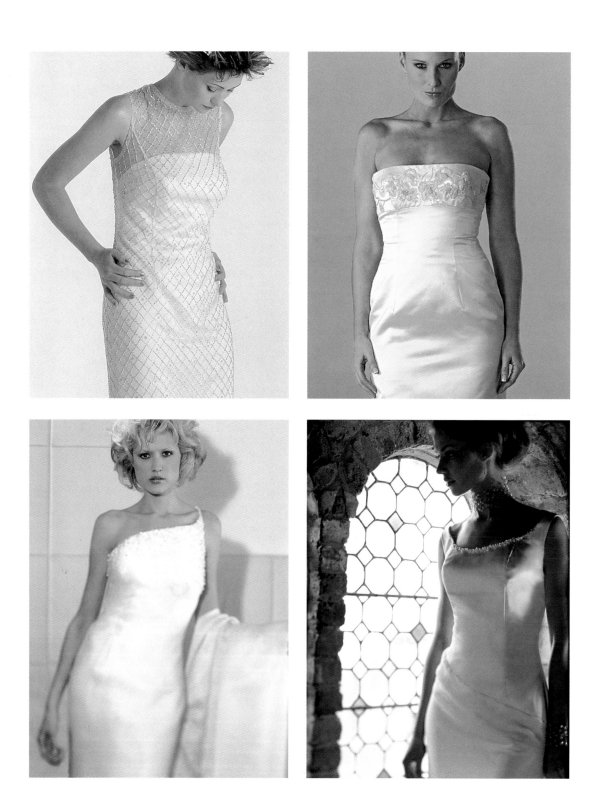

OPPOSITE 1930's inspired white gown with a clever twist and Watteau train in chiffon.
ABOVE, CLOCKWISE FROM TOP LEFT Added sparkle – silver bugle bead lattice on a simple sleeveless
organza column over a strapless base; Stewart Parvin designed cream strapless column with
sequin and beaded floral border; draped skirt on a princess line column with beaded scoop
neckline; asymmetric neckline scattered with beads on this modern dress style.

LEFT A simple sheath in dramatic ribbon lace with scalloped hem and satin straps.

OPPOSITE Antonia Pugh-Thomas design in lace over a white shantung silk underlay.

OPPOSITE The beautiful decorative edge of this cascading veil sets off a simple ivory strapless column with motif at the bustline.

ABOVE RIGHT V-neck column in silk crepe, with split skirt and floral trim by Antonia Pugh-Thomas.

BELOW RIGHT This modern split skirted design has ruffled edges and an empire line embroidered bodice.

MINI AND MIDI

MINI AND MIDI

The minidress denotes anything that falls above the knee, and so can include many of the contemporary slip and shift dresses that are available today, as well as miniskirt suits and a few oddities like the puffball. A mididress falls just below the knee.

HISTORY

The mini is a 1960's icon, like Twiggy and the Beatles it is synonymous with the era. Free love and the sexual revolution were seen as a herald for personal expression and with them a new self-confident generation whose body image defined the generation gap. The development of more practical underwear as tights replaced stockings and suspenders may also have had a part to play.

Courrèges, Paco Rabanne and Pierre Cardin all experimented with shorter A-line styles in 1964-5, but it was not until 1966 that the style really took off. Mary Quant raised the hemlines high above the knee, and combined with op-art graphics and Vidal Sassoon's geometric cut the look became the definitive style for 60's swinging London.

The 1980's revival of short added another dimension – tight. Azzedine Alaia's micro mini stretch lycra knits on leggy supermodels, and Vivienne Westwood's ironic mini-crinis and puffball style skirts were sexy pastiches of the cumbersome nineteenth century creations. As the cult of youth prevails, the mini enjoys a perennial appeal, rather than shocking it is just a familiar part of our vocabulary of dress.

CLASSICS

A strapless mini sheath can look stunning if you have the figure to carry it off. A minidress teamed with a suit jacket, like Mia Farrow's outfit to wed Sinatra looks simple and stylish with her elfish crop, as does a slip or shift dress which falls just above the knee. Team with a sheer wrap or a cocoon coat for a covered up appearance.

WHO SHOULD WEAR

Only slim and athletic builds need apply for shorter styles. Ideal for petite figures, but not necessarily those who are very skinny. The knee length shift styles are more flattering if you are more curvy. Remember that it needs to be an appropriate choice for the type and location of the ceremony. Some brides choose to have detachable panels which they can remove, transforming a full length to a mini for the reception.

FABRICS

Just about anything goes for a mini style, it will just depend on the weight and construction you choose. If it is a stiffer A-line mini then choose more heavyweights like faille, gabardine or textured pique. Damask, brocade and chunky lace give texture, while 60's dresses were often made from wool jerseys and softer overlaid fabrics.

LEFT In a dress to match her hair colour, pop star and TV hostess Cilla Black (Priscilla White) at her 1969 wedding to her manager Bobby Willis at Marylebone registry office.

OPPOSITE, CLOCKWISE FROM TOP LEFT Mini stars: second time around, Audrey Hepburn goes short in a space-age funnel-necked creation; Frank Sinatra's third wife, Mia Farrow, wears a pale silk cropped jacket over a mini dress; Cilla (for her religious ceremony in Liverpool, 1969) chooses another minidress, this time in white, and trimmed with maribou feathers and a belt; actress Sharon Tate wears a moiré puff sleeved minidress with beaded trim as she cuts the cake with film director husband Roman Polanski.

OPPOSITE Chanel provided a lead for the new short lengths
becoming fashionable for weddings in the 1920s. This dress is
worn by Countess Von Bismarck, 1925.

ABOVE Midi length prom style with petticoats in this 1950's
vintage dress.

OPPOSITE Another 1950's inspired dress in this modern champagne duchess satin midi-length shift with belt by Antonia Pugh-Thomas.

ABOVE RIGHT On the runway at Vera Wang, 2003, this strapless minidress with rich embroidery is given a pretty detail with its cream ribbon belt.

BELOW RIGHT Another Vera Wang creation, this modern dress features pearlescent sequins in an oversized lace pattern on a sheer minidress over an ivory slip.

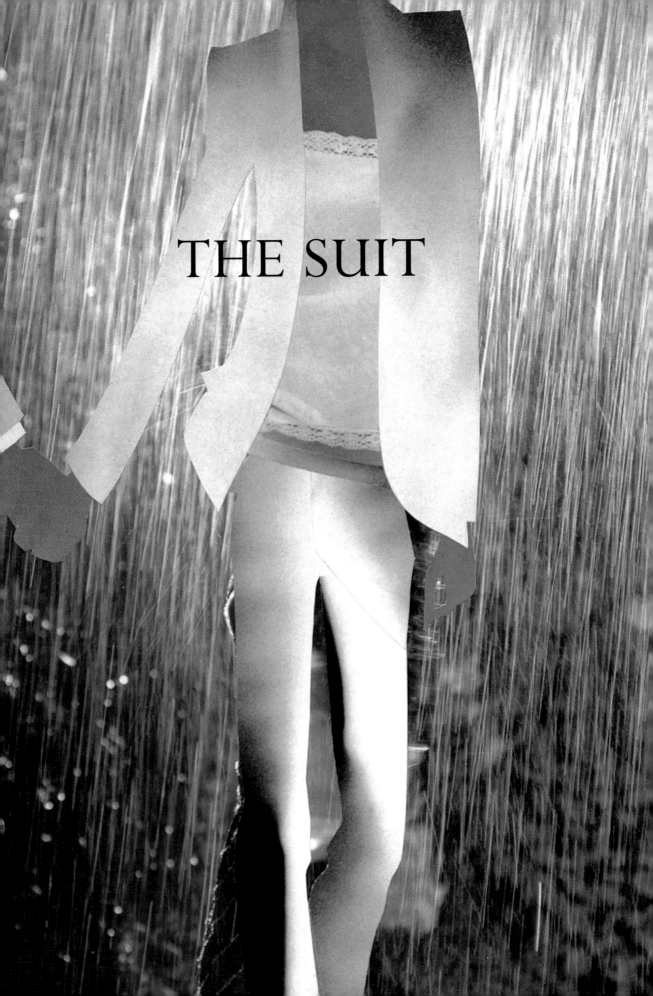

THE SUIT

THE SUIT

STYLE

The suit is a two-piece outfit, consisting of a jacket and trousers or skirt. Bianca's wedding to Mick Jagger in a white trouser suit is the archetypal image which comes to mind. But she wasn't actually wearing trousers, it was a skirt! So whether you wear the trousers or not is up to you, there are a number of stylish variations on the two-piece outfit which can work well. Suits are more practical if you want to zoom in and out of the registry office, or you are just the kind of person who doesn't want to wear a dress, and they offer the freedom to dress up and down, with or without a train, veil or gloves. There is also an increase in the number of people who for ethical or practical reasons want wearability from what they choose, and do not want to consign their outfit to the loft once the big day is over. The advantage of wearing a two-piece outfit is that you can wear it again piecemeal, and it also offers a lot more off-the-peg choice.

HISTORY

Historically only courtiers and royal brides would have specially created gowns for their wedding ceremony, and the majority of couples would simply don their best outfit for their special day. It was not until the wartime era of the 1940s which saw many brides opting again, out of necessity, to simply wear their best suit to be married in. Rationing of fabrics and scarcity of bridal materials added to the rarity of full wedding dresses, other than heirlooms and those borrowed from friends and family members. Post-war saw a return to romantic dressing-up, but the more liberal post-war attitudes to dress and the increase in civil ceremonies and second marriages has contributed to the popularity of the suit as an alternative to the traditional dress. The cultural revolution of the 1960s also saw the suit take on a new role, either overtly sexual (mini, hot pants) or androgynous blurring of the genders where couples wore "his and hers", matching suits *á la* Serge Gainsbourg and Jane Birkin (*Je t'aime*)…

Yves Saint Laurent's "Le Smoking", a cinch-waisted take on the tuxedo, never looked more predatory than on Charlotte Rampling or the women of Helmut Newton's fashion spreads of the 1970s. By the 1980s the suit became the exaggerated, wide-shouldered symbol of the power dressing working woman, typified by designers like Montana and Mugler. The style has moved away from those cartoon excesses now and is present in the collections of a myriad of designers who understand what women want from tailoring. Armani and Yamamoto are extremely skilled in soft unstructured tailoring which retains a sense of femininity, while Jil Sander and Helmut Lang offer more modern architectural looks.

CLASSICS

The white tux evening suit *à la* YSL is the classic masculine take on the suit. A softer shawl-collared jacket worn with wider palazzo pants may be more forgiving and the Chanel style skirt suit is a feminine alternative. A strapless basque top and trousers can work with or without a jacket, and long line Edwardian jackets over full, floor length skirts, or coatdresses offer more elegant solutions. There are lots of detail options, such as collar and sleeve types, peplums and trims. If you are getting married in a more exotic location, you might consider a more harmonious solution such as a kaftan top or crochet tunic with trousers – even a bikini. The birthday suit is the obvious choice for the naturist ceremony, and will save many hours of deliberation!

WHO SHOULD WEAR

If you want to wear a suit then you will always be able to find one which will flatter your figure. It is more about your persona than your figure when it comes to wearing a suit. Just like a ball gown, the construction of a jacket is such that it can flatter and disguise any problem areas of your body. Short waist length jackets can proportion petite figures. Long line jackets, or a peplum style with nipped waist can help shape a straight up and down silhouette. If you are curvy, then often a shorter style, like the ones shown on Liz Taylor and Marilyn Monroe (see pages 134-5) will draw emphasis to your waist. Full skirt and Edwardian flared equestrian style jackets will flatter the pear shaped figure.

FABRICS

So many options here it will depend entirely on the type of suit you decide on. Aside from the usual silks there is much more choice available in a two-piece outfit – from crisp white linen to chunky wool bouclé and silk tweed for traditional suits, to cool cotton voile or habotai silk for a floaty kaftan style. Gaberdines and grosgrains have a twill or rib that adds texture, as do jacquards, damasks and other decorative weave structures which can add another dimension to a simple cut.

OPPOSITE Elizabeth Taylor in grey Dior style full skirt and waisted jacket for her marriage to Michael Wilding, 1952.
ABOVE, CLOCKWISE FROM TOP LEFT Bianca's infamous YSL skirt suit worn to wed Rolling Stones lead singer Mick Jagger,
1971; Marilyn Monroe wore a demure dark brown suit trimmed with ermine to marry Joe DiMaggio, 1954; actress
Amanda Barry's pale trouser suit for her 1967 wedding; a headband adds the finishing touch to model Bronwen Pugh's
outfit for her 1960 wedding to Lord Astor.

OPPOSITE This long line gunmetal silk jacket with oriental embroidered organza overlay is more of a coatdress than a classic suit, but is perfect for a registry office wedding or for the bride who doesn't feel that a huge white dress is appropriate.

ABOVE RIGHT His and Hers — off-the-peg suits make for a practical alternative you can wear again. Here the bride sets hers apart from day wear by wearing a statement vintage necklace.

BELOW RIGHT Strident style in this white satin 1970's inspired tuxedo jacket and trousers with beaded detail by Johanna Hehir. It is set off by a contemporary white feather hairpiece.

LEFT Clean and stylish in a 1970's inspired trouser suit with generous lapels and flared trousers. This is a fun, modern look that is also timeless.

NECKLINES

NECKLINES

The silhouette of a dress, and the impact it has on the viewer are as much dictated by the neckline as by any other detail on the dress. It is the focal point which helps to frame the face and should be harmonious with the physique of the wearer. As the neckline exposes or covers the neck and shoulders, and the amount of décolletage, it is important for details such as jewellery and accessories, as well as enhancing your own features. If you have great coathanger shoulders and collarbone which you want to show, then a strapless style is a good option, but off-the-shoulder, halter or asymmetric styles could also be great alternatives. Here is a glossary of styles.

STRAPLESS
The strapless style bodice cuts straight across the body at the underarm, although it may curve up or down as it passes across the bust. Often a two layer or cut-away will suggest more than is revealed, and lace trim, ruffled or silk floral decorations are applied at the break. Good for strong athletic shoulders and arms, and the simple style allows for ostentatious jewellery, gloves and big hair. Very flat chested and heavier set upper body shapes are best to avoid this style.

SWEETHEART
An alternative strapless style, as the name suggests this curves across the bust into a central V. While the straight cut is suitable for a smaller to medium bust, the sweetheart allows more room for corset construction and a larger bust for more Jayne Mansfield proportioned cleavage. Can be set into a sheer or lace fabric which rises to a high or simple round neck, giving the illusion of cleavage without putting it in anyone's face, and also giving additional support.

DROP SHOULDER
An off-the-shoulder line which sweeps across the body to bands on the upper arm. These can be simple or gathered and puffed like a sleeve. The effect is broadening and good for exposing neck and collarbone. If you already have broad shoulders you will not need the extra this style gives. A good style for balancing the pear shaped silhouette, and consequently to avoid if you have no hips.

PORTRAIT COLLAR
An alternate version of the drop shoulder, reminiscent of the 1950s. The collar folds over itself to reveal the neck and shoulders. An elegant and useful style which at once reveals and conceals. Good to accentuate necks and collarbones, also to minimize a large bust and emphasize the waist.

HALTER NECK

Usually with backless or low backed styles, the halter is a strap which passes from front armhole or bust point around the back neck to the opposite front, like a bikini strap. This gives support to a dress front, and is good for both maximizing a smaller bust and supporting a larger one. Not advisable if you require additional bra support.

COWL NECK

A draped style with swathed fabric which scoops across the bust. Often found in 1950's style and bias cut dresses. Good for disguising a small bust and adding interest at the neckline. Not good for a large bust.

SPAGHETTI STRAP

Delicate straps, often in multiples, which may be just decorative on corset type bodices, or suspend bias and slip dresses. Good for small, but not advisable for large busts.

BOAT NECK

Skims the collar bone to meet at the shoulder point, another style reminiscent of the 1950s and associated with the shift dress. Ideal for petite and flat chested figures, but not suitable for anyone with much bust as the line is easily distorted.

ROUND NECK

T-shirt style neckline which is good for those not so confident about exposing a lot of skin. A favourite with many modern designers, as it can be imaginatively embellished. As with a T-shirt this style is better suited to a smaller bust.

SCOOP NECK

A more daring vest style neckline which can dip as low as you dare, and is suitable for anyone who is happy with their chest and neck to be exposed.

V-NECK

Like the scoop but dipping to a point, the V elongates the neck and is flattering to a medium bust, but not so great for large or small busts.

SQUARE NECK

A deep square scoop neckline usually associated with empire line and corset styles. This can help minimize a large bust, but is suitable for most shapes.

HIGH NECK

Various styles available, from stand collars like Nehru and Mandarin which abut at the throat to high button and shirt collar types. Good for covering up the neck and chest and an elongated silhouette. Suitable for all except where the neck would be a problem.

OPPOSITE A Caroline Parkes design with shoulder point neckline on an ivory beaded lace bodice.
ABOVE, CLOCKWISE FROM TOP LEFT Sheer roundneck over a strapless dress; asymmetric neckline
on an interesting spiral cut dress with silver lace and brooch motif at the strap; this
halterneck-collared dress with sequinned bodice shows off square shoulders;
1950's style boat-neck dress in cream by Stewart Parvin.

LEFT Cowl neck champagne silk dress, with pearl bead-filled crumb catcher.

OPPOSITE Square neck dress with shaped straps. The embroidered bodice is dotted with diamante and crystal beads and stones to match the necklace.

ABOVE LEFT Square neck with spaghetti straps overlaid with lace by Caroline Parkes.

BELOW LEFT Shallow scooped neckline to the shoulder point helps emphasize the collar bone in this Caroline Parkes design.

OPPOSITE A very simple V-neck design, which could be set off with a statement necklace.

ABOVE LEFT Draped cowl-neck dress with turquoise print.

BOTTOM LEFT Sweetheart neckline trimmed with silk roses on a corset bodice.

BOTTOM RIGHT Minimal style with a square strapless neckline.

OPPOSITE Classic portrait collar on an off-the-shoulder dress by Stewart Parvin.

BACKS

OPPOSITE Bias cut crepe dress with cowl back and cross-over spaghetti straps by designer Sarah Owen. A sophisticated design.

RIGHT Butterflies rest on the cross back detail of this nature inspired dress.

OPPOSITE This romantic leaf-patterned Phillipa Lepley design is crowned at the back with a large cascading organza flower corsage. BELOW, CLOCKWISE FROM TOP LEFT Caroline Parkes ribboned corsetry detail on the back of a strapless gown; diamante laces criss-cross and sparkle in a deep cowl backed dress; lavender and ivory shades in this oriental inspired floral obi are held with decorative chopsticks; white silk roses clasp the waist at the back of this dress.

LEFT A delicate lace camisole top trimmed in satin and with covered buttons to match the dress is cut away below the bust with a scalloped edge.

OPPOSITE A more dramatic approach with this antique white ballgown which has cut away and appliqué beading to create a lace effect at the back.

SLEEVES

SLEEVES

Whether you opt for sleeves or not will depend on the style of dress, and how happy you are to be exposing your arms. Remember you can use gloves, a wrap and veil to good effect too, particularly if you must cover up to satisfy the dictates of the ceremony. Sleeves can add dramatic counterpoint to your dress style, and sheer or lace sleeves can camouflage, elongate and flatter your silhouette. While you may want to consider the season and location of your wedding, the inspiration should really be dictated by the dress style. If you want to create maximum impact in your fairytale ball gown then you will want to opt for an off-the-shoulder, balloon or "leg o'mutton" style. An Empire dress will best suit capped and slim fitted styles, while a minidress will want a flared or T-shirt style to be sympathetic. That is not to say that you cannot mix and match, the only rule should be is that if it looks right it is right. So if you usually wear a vest top, a kaftan or a skinny rib sweater then you will know what suits you best.

OFF-THE-SHOULDER
More like broad straps, or puffed bands which are just attached at the underarm to give an alluring bare shouldered silhouette. Best with fitted bodice styles of dress, but can add width so beware if you are very broad shouldered.

CAP
A close fitting sleeve which caps the shoulder, often found on shift-style 1950's dresses. Softer versions, which may be gathered onto a band, or in several sheer layers for Empire styles. Best for showing off well toned arms, and teamed with opera-length gloves.

SHORT
T-shirt style sleeves which will suit most styles of dress. Good for camouflaging upper arms.

TULIP
Short sleeve comprising petal shaped overlap. A more delicate short sleeve style usually in sheer fabrics.

ELBOW
An elbow length sleeve which is usually slim fitting, but may have a cuff or band at the hem. Sometimes shaped or cut away.

THREE-QUARTER
Cut between the elbow and the wrist, this length can be slimming if your arms are not so toned, it should finish at the narrowest point on the arm to give an elongated effect.

LONG
Long slim sleeves are great for lace and sheer fabrics, giving the illusion of an exposed arm while keeping you covered. Lace scalloped edges, cuffs and bound edges can give an added dimension.

PUFF
There are several variations on puffed sleeves, depending on the amount of volume in the sleeve, and where it is cut. Juliet sleeves have a small puff at the shoulder, and continue as a long slim sleeve. "Leg o' mutton" or Balloon sleeves puff to the elbow and are slim to the wrist (see page 169), while the Poet sleeve is full from shoulder to wrist.

BELL
The opposite to the puff is the bell, which is slim to the elbow, flaring gently to the wrist.

KIMONO
Kimono sleeves are deep and wide Oriental-style rectangular sleeves, often cut into the body of the dress.

CAPE
Circular sleeves usually cut in soft or sheer fabrics which are gathered onto the shoulder and fall in a cascade to any length. Very "*Abigails Party*" (see page 171).

OPPOSITE Audrey Hepburn's puff sleeves are tucked into skin-tight elbow length gloves.
ABOVE, CLOCKWISE FROM TOP LEFT Sheer capped sleeves on a dress at the Wedding March on
Madison, New York, 2003; Crown Princess Mary of Denmark wears split elbow length sleeves in
her wedding gown by Danish designer Uffe Frank, 2004; cream crepe brocade dress with drop
shoulder flared sleeves; short T-Shirt style sleeves in an off-white princess line dress with bow.

OPPOSITE Pin tucked and draped handkerchief sleeves on a dress by designer Sarah Owen.
BELOW Zandra Rhodes inspired sheer ruched cape sleeves on a pale empire line dress.

ABOVE RIGHT Beaded detatchable cap sleeves on a dress by Australian designer Maggie Sottero.

BELOW RIGHT This straight satin "Charlotte" gown by Phillipa Lepley, is set apart by the silk tulle fluted bell-shaped sleeves, with appliquéd Chantilly lace flowers.

OPPOSITE Princess Grace kneels to show the exquisite detail of her rose point lace fitted sleeves embroidered with tiny pearls.

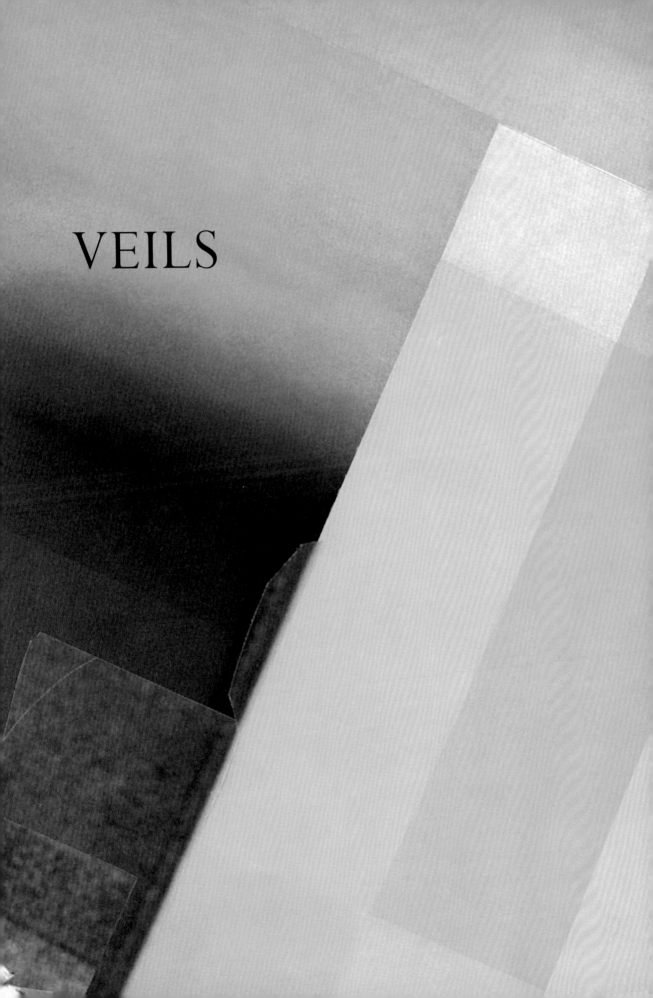

VEILS

VEILS

Roman brides wore veils, known as "*flammeum*" which were dyed a golden shade with saffron to represent the flame of Vesta, the domestic goddess and giver of life. The veil was to protect the bride from evil spirits and was a symbol of her betrothal for life.

The introduction of the veil into Europe seems to have come from the Middle East, brought back by knights from the crusades. In these arranged marriages it was used to hide the bride's face from the groom who would not have hitherto seen her. Once they were married the groom was allowed to unveil his new wife's face, at which point it was too late for any second thoughts. This may be the reasoning behind the Jewish tradition where the groom checks to see if the bride is the girl of his choosing before placing the veil over her head.

Fashions for the veil waxed and waned, and it was not until Queen Victoria's wedding that the fashion for veils was firmly cemented once again. The modern veil has evolved through the past century, as new materials and fashions have impacted on the styles. So when it comes to choosing there are a variety of styles and details to choose from. Traditional lace, soft sheer or stiff nylon tulle, multiple layers to the floor and short styles can be worn with a number of headpieces or hats.

You may have an heirloom veil that has been passed down through the generations, or you may choose to have a new veil, trimmed with your dress fabric. Whatever you decide, just remember that it must be sympathetic to your dress in style and colour, and comply with any stipulations there may be with your religious ceremony. If you are wearing a veil that will cover your face during the ceremony, it is important to get the attachment right, and the headpiece which will work for this – have a practice before the day. Otherwise have fun with it, it may be the only time in your life you wear one.

BLUSHER

A short shoulder length style which is fixed atop the head so it can easily be pushed back over the head during the ceremony. Best for simple modern dress styles and suits. Will suit all face shapes.

ELBOW

As the name suggests, a simple veil that falls to the elbow. These include Fountain styles which may be multiple layers of fabric gathered at the crown, either softly cascading, or in stiffer fabrics to create added height and shape. Good for thin faces as the height and width will help reproportion the face.

FINGERTIP

A veil which reaches to the fingertips, it is a classic veil length, often trimmed in lace or satin ribbon. If you are not so slim, be careful that this style doesn't add width to your waist visually.

WALTZ

A calf or ankle length veil which will usually be a softer style. Good for rounder face shapes as it will help to slim and elongate.

CHAPEL

A more traditional style of veil, often worn with ballgowns. The chapel veil just sweeps the floor, and may cascade in several layers. Often worn at the back of the head it can help balance a long or thin face. May be worn with a blusher.

CATHEDRAL

The longest and most formal style, usually seen in royal weddings. The veil will fall as a train behind the wearer.

MANTILLA

Spanish style lace veil which encases the wearer from top to toe, and falls from the crown of the head. Will work beautifully with simple column or mermaid styles.

ABOVE LEFT Caught in the moment – a bride adjusts her tiered fountain veil.

BELOW LEFT An elbow length veil in white net is secured with a tiara.

OPPOSITE Mantilla style lace trimmed veil by Spanish designer Rosa Clara.

ABOVE RIGHT Martha Boss, a top US bridal model, wears a nylon tulle lace gown and veil.

BELOW RIGHT In contrast, this soft net chapel length veil falls gently to the floor.

OPPOSITE Fingertip veil with edge trim and embroidered border.

ABOVE, CLOCKWISE FROM TOP LEFT A fountain veil falls at the back of the head; blusher style with satin trim worn by Mexican actress and singer Thalia for her wedding to Tommy Mottola, 2000; black on black, a model wears a black Oscar de la Renta wedding dress with beaded net veil; an alternative to the traditional veil is this wrapped style veil which encases the head OPPOSITE A cathedral length veil trails behind a model showing a dress by Spanish designer Rosa Clara.

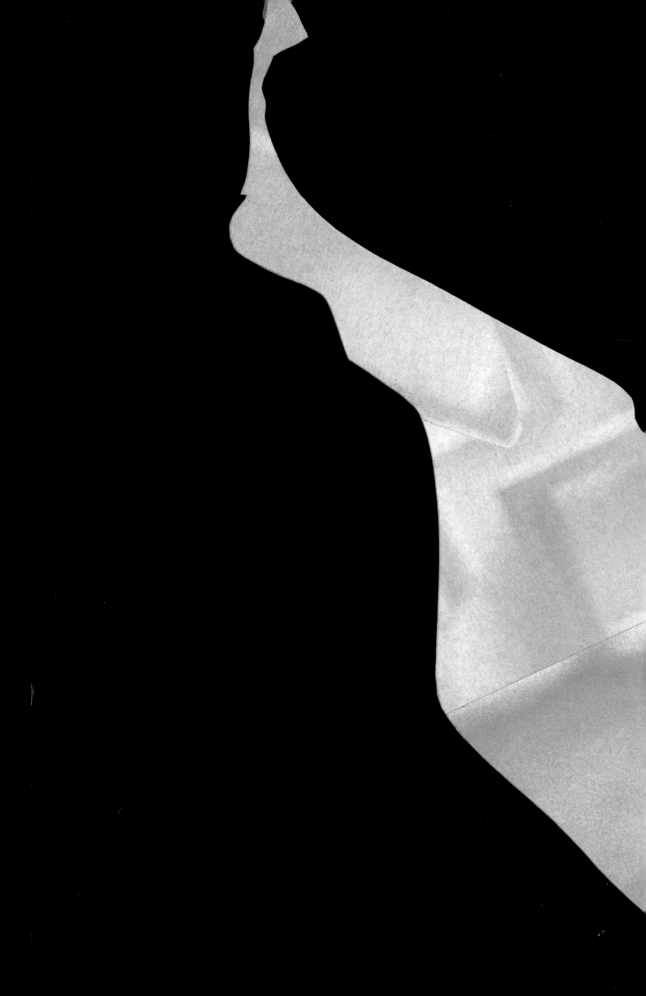

LEFT Letizia of Spain in a Manuel Pertegaz dress with a 15 foot long royal train embroidered with heraldic symbols, at her wedding to Crown Prince Felipe of Spain, 2004.

OPPOSITE Gloria Swanson as Princess Marie in the 1924 film *Her Love Story*, wears a dress with a richly decorated royal train trimmed in ermine.

ABOVE RIGHT Vintage 1960's wedding dress with panel train.

BELOW RIGHT An Antonia Pugh-Thomas design with circular cathedral train falling 7 feet from the waist.

DETAILS

HEADWEAR

If you are going to wear a veil, then you will need something to keep it in place on your head. This may be a simple band or comb, or a floral garland. Orange blossom is traditionally associated with the bride going back to the Romans. Queen Victoria re-established the tradition by wearing a garland of orange blossom for her wedding – subsequently real and imitation silk orange blossom has remained a popular tradition for brides. You might want to match your bouquet, dress fabric or corsage with a floral headpiece, or you may decide on an alternative statement piece or hat without a veil.

Decide if you are a hair, a veil or a hat person. If you are wearing your veil to the front for the ceremony, your headpiece may have to be limited in size and type. If you are wearing a lace or decorated veil you may not want to detract from it with any additional headwear. If you are wearing your veil to the back, and your hair is more important then you may just want to keep it as the focus. Hair that is piled up on top of your head may benefit from a simple ribbon to match the dress, or dotted with decorative hairpins or floral sprigs. If you have shorter hair you might want to wear a hat – wide brimmed and top hats with veils wrapped or draped over them entirely can look striking with the right dress or suit. Tiny pillbox hats with short veils which just cover the eyes can be a seductive partner to 1950's styles, while headbands and feather creations team well with shorter 1920's styles and modern columns. Make sure you look at the whole picture when deciding, so trying on a hat without the dress is not such a good idea.

OPPOSITE This dramatic pillbox hat with spiral feather quills looks like a miniature wedding cake. The lace matches the dress by designer Antonia Pugh-Thomas. The hat is by Katharine Goodison Millinery.

OPPOSITE A feather headdress frames a simple crop hairstyle, and matches a waist detail.

ABOVE LEFT Only for the adventurous – a nylon tulle veil adorns a wide brimmed hat by Torrente Haute Couture, 2001.

BELOW LEFT Vintage finishing touches – a matching hat finishes the outfit as a bride steps from the car. Ideal for a registry office wedding.

BELOW RIGHT Decorative hairpins add the finishing detail to a basketweave hairstyle.

PREVIOUS PAGE, LEFT A statement headpiece is an alternative to a veil, this silk floral peony compliments the embroidery on the dress.

PREVIOUS PAGE, RIGHT The lattice net of this short "fascinator" veil is secured with a silk rose.

OPPOSITE The natural look – a garland of real flowers is a pretty complement to the bridal bouquet in this SaraSusa design.

RIGHT The fresh green of a simple band of ivy sets of this romantic white ensemble.

JEWELLERY

An alternative to floral headpieces and hats is something more delicate and sparkly. Tiaras and crowns in particular play a part in some traditional wedding ceremonies. Aside from the royal connotations associated with crowns and brides, there are associations with Adam and Eve, the king and queen of creation, and in some Scandinavian and Russian Orthodox ceremonies a crown is placed on the bride's head. Half crowns and tiaras are more popular and more practical. They vary in size and complexity from small barrette styles to regal arcs which work well with a bun, securing a veil with a little added glitter.

A strapless gown can be a foil for a stunning crystal choker, and if your dress is being scattered with pearls or beads you might pick up these details with your accessories. If you are wearing an heirloom piece, or something you have been given for your engagement, you might choose this as the starting point and develop your dress and accessories around it. Your star signs have symbolic colours, stones and metals which you might choose to link to your jewellery theme, as certain crystals and colours have associated powers and superstitions. If you are wearing a period style then details, like the style of headband, bracelet or choker appropriate to the style of dress can add an authentic touch. Keep it simple and don't overdo it – one strong piece with a simple column dress can look stunning, you will reduce the effect with matching earrings, bracelet, anklet, belly chain and toe rings. Save this look for a beach wedding in Ibiza.

OPPOSITE A delicate diamante studded
tiara sets off a sleek hairstyle.

OPPOSITE A tiara adds sparkle to a mass of curls, worn with a simple pearl bracelet.

RIGHT, CLOCKWISE FROM TOP LEFT Varying tiara styles: a half crown; a matching necklace and headband-style tiara; Pre-Raphaelite-style floral band; decorative hairpins or slides hold long hair in place; a discreet barette-style tiara; an ornate decorative comb keeps hair in place for a swept up style.

BELOW, CLOCKWISE FROM TOP LEFT Crystal beads and feathers make an interesting armlet cuff,
matching amethyst necklace and earrings; crystal beading on the dress is picked up with a
matching diamante bracelet; a twinkling multistrand necklace complements a strapless gown.
OPPOSITE A classic set of pearls is hard to beat for a demure, vintage look.

BEADING AND DECORATION

There are two schools when it comes to embellishing dresses — less is more and more is more. Traditionally, conspicuous consumption was the driving force behind much of the decoration of gowns, with precious metal threads, beads and furs used to trim the gown and signify the status of the wearer and her family. Today the addition of embroidery, lace, appliqué, beading, sequins and fabric flowers, feathers and tassels is down to personal taste. These details are what can make your dress a personal statement, and it can be a great way to customise something you buy off-the-peg: many trims and motifs can be bought individually or on the roll and applied by machine or hand. Beading, embroidery and sequins on the other hand, can be highly skilled crafts, and take considerable time to apply, so if you are having a dress made seek advice from your maker at the start if you plan to have this kind of detail. Often the embellishment will have to be applied before construction of the dress is completed.

BORDERS/TRIM
Edge bindings, braiding or ribbons are used to give a decorative or contrasting edge. Lace, feathers or ruffles give softness particularly on strapless bodices and hems.

MOTIFS
A placed design which may be small on a bodice, or large as a feature on backs and trains. May be embroidered, beaded, appliquéd or use combinations of effects.

SPRIG/SCATTER
Small motifs scattered evenly over the dress. Good for simpler column and slip styles

CASCADE
A large motif which appears to wrap or cascade down the body. May be asymmetrical. Good for all styles.

INSERT/CUT OUT
Usually lace or sheer motifs which are cut into the body of the dress. This also applies to larger panels which may frame the bust or hem a sleeve or train. Good for all styles.

ALL OVER
Usually applied to the bodice of a dress where beading or sequins give a striking contrast between the upper and lower parts. Good with ballgown and empire styles.

OPPOSITE Shimmering gauze flowers scatter asymmetrically across this Caroline Parkes design.
ABOVE, CLOCKWISE FROM TOP LEFT Embroidery and appliqué add modesty to a revealing slip
dress; fly-away feather collar and cuffs finish a sheer knit top; a mass of appliqué silk flowers
adorn the neckline and strap of a striking blue dress; silk petals follow the line of a plunging back.

ABOVE LEFT Bugle beads trace lines across the bodice and skirt of this dress in a modern design.

ABOVE RIGHT Traditional eastern motifs are embroidered in black on this exquisite velvet dress, worn by actress Katherine Hepburn for her 1928 wedding to Ogden Smith.

LEFT Diamante net is overlaid on the bodice of this sparkling dress by Lebanese designer Pierre Katra, 2004.

OPPOSITE Jewel encrusted – the heavily sequinned bodice of this dress contrasts with the simple wrapped silk skirt.

A FINAL WORD ON ACCESSORIES…

All those little personal details which take time and patience to finish your outfit, from the right gloves or shoes, to the perfume you wear, can be so rewarding – making your day an experience for you and your partner which is more intimate within the bigger picture of the wedding itself. It could be down to your entwined initials embroidered into the lining, or a favourite colour or shared experience that you choose to reference. I remember making a dress for a bride whose partner had lost both his parents, and she asked for a pocket to be made in the interior of the dress so that she could carry a picture of them so that they wouldn't miss the big day. These finishing touches can be the most rewarding and enduring memories of your wedding day, so are well worth the extra effort.

OPPOSITE Personal details – an antique
purse and embroidered choker set off
a stunning laser-cut organza skirt and
chenille wrap by Robinson Valentine.

BELOW, CLOCKWISE FROM TOP LEFT Finishing touches – French actress Bridget Bardot finishes her outfit with a muff for her 1952 wedding; a capelet can offer warmth and modesty for a church; or add interest like this Vera Wang wrap in shredded tulle; add a sequinned and beaded bag to match the dress, and hold all the last minute essentials. OPPOSITE Getting it right on the day – this bride is taking no chances with the weather in an Antonia Pugh-Thomas dress and wellington boots.

Above all remember to have fun!

INDEX

accessories 216–219
a-line dresses 92–107
appliqué 210–13

backs 152–163
    corsage 154, 160–61
    corsetry 154, 161
    covered buttons 154, 156, 157
    draped 154, 161
    lace insert 154, 162, 163
    V-back 154
    X-back 154, 158, 159
bags 218
ball gowns 12–31
Bardot, Bridget 218
beading 210–219
bias-cut 158–59, 70–71
Black, Cilla 124–25

capes 218
Caroline Castigliano Collection
    40–1
Clara, Rosa 178–79, 182–83
coatdress 136–37
column dresses 108–119

decoration 210–219
details 194–219
    accessories 216–219
    beading 210–219
    decoration 210–219
    headwear 196–203
    jewellery 204–209
Diana, Princess of Wales 15, 17,
    187

Electra, Carmen 37
empire-line dresses 52–67

Farrow, Mia 122, 124–25
fishtail dresses 68–91
    see also Mermaid dresses
floral garland 196, 200, 202, 203

Goodison, Katharine 196–7

hair 196
headwear 196–203
Heche, Anne 72–3
Hehir, Johanna 137
Hepburn, Audrey 55, 95, 96,
    124–25, 168–69
Hepburn, Katherine 214

Jagger, Bianca 132, 134
Jenks, Cozmo 80-1

jewellery 204–209

Katra, Pierre 214
Kelly, Grace 15, 17, 172–73

Lanvin, Jeanne 59
Lepley, Phillipa 18, 28, 66,
    160–61, 172
Letizia of Spain 190–91
Lomba, Modesto 188, 189
Lopez, Jennifer 95, 96–7

Mary of Denmark 168
McQueen, Alexander 57
mermaid dresses 68–91
    see also Fishtail dresses
midi dresses 120–129
millinery 196
mini dresses 120–129
Mischka, Badgley 37
Monroe, Marilyn 111, 134
Mortimer, Emily 55, 57

necklaces 204, 208, 209
necklines 140–151
    boat 143, 145
    cowl 143, 146, 150
    drop shoulder 142
    halter 143, 145
    high 143
    portrait collar 142, 150–51
    round 143, 145
    scoop 143, 149
    spaghetti straps 143
    square 143, 146–47, 149, 150
    strapless 142, 150
    sweetheart 142, 150
    V-neck 143, 148

Oscar de la Renta 182
Owen, Sarah 67, 90–1, 106–7,
    158–59, 170–71

Parkes, Caroline 40, 44, 47, 50,
    63, 98–9, 106, 144–45,
    149, 161, 187
Parvin, Stewart 47, 78, 84, 114,
    145, 150–51
Pertegaz, Manuel 190–91
princess-line dresses 32–51
Pugh-Thomas, Antonia 74, 106,
    116–17, 119, 128–29, 193,
    196–97, 218–19

Queen Elizabeth II 35, 36–7

Richards, Denise 71, 73

SaraSusa 29, 37, 112–13, 202
sleeves 164–173
    bell 167, 172
    cap 166, 168, 172
    cape 167, 171
    elbow 167, 168
    handkerchief 170–71
    kimono 167
    long 167, 172–73
    off-the-shoulder 166, 168
    puff 167, 168–69
    short 166, 168
    three quarter 167
    tulip 167
Sophie of Wessex 71, 72
Sottero, Maggie 172
suits 130–139
Swanson, Gloria 192, 193

Tate, Sharon 124–25
Taylor, Elizabeth 15, 16–17,
    134–35
tiaras 204, 205, 206, 207
Todd, Elizabeth 22
Torrente Haute Couture 198
trains 184–193
    brush 187, 188
    cathedral 186, 187, 193
    chapel 186, 187, 188
    court 187
    detachable 186
    panel 187, 188, 193
    royal 187, 190-91, 192, 193
    watteau 187
Tyler, Liv 55, 57

Valentine, Robinson 216–17
Valentino 95, 96–7
veils 174–183, 187, 196, 201
    blusher 177, 182
    cathedral 177, 182–83
    chapel 177
    elbow 177, 178
    fingertip 177, 180–81
    fountain 178, 182
    mantilla 177, 178–79
    waltz 177
vintage 26–7, 57, 58, 59, 101,
    112, 126–27, 193, 198, 209

Wang, Vera 129, 218
Winslet, Kate 55, 56–7

Yves Saint Laurent 132, 133, 134

DIRECTORY

Caroline Castigliano Collection
www.carolinecastigliano.co.uk
Bridalwear—off-the-rack and bespoke
Stores throughout the UK

Fredek Designs
155 Seymour Place
London
W1H 5GT
Tel: +44 (0) 20 7723 2573
Dressmaking service

Katharine Goodison Millinery
93 Winchester Street
London
SW1V 4NX
Tel: +44 (0) 20 7828 6498
Bridal millinery
By appointment only

Leigh Goodsell Photography
Tel: +44 (0) 20 7613 2188/
+44 (0) 1485 210 841
www.goodsell.ws
Wedding photography
Potrait commissions include
HRH Prince Charles

Johanna Hehir
10/12 Chiltern Street
London
W1U 7PX
Tel: +44 (0) 20 7486 2760
www.johanna-hehir.com
Made-to-measure modern bridalwear

Cozmo Jenks
21 New Quebec Street
London W1H 7SA
Tel: +44 (0) 20 7258 0111
www.cozmojenks.co.uk
Bridal headpieces and millinery

Pierre Katra
PO Box 60137
Jal El Dib, Lebanon
www.pierrekatra.com
Designer bridalwear

Phillipa Lepley
494 Fulham Road
London
SW6 5NH
Tel: +44 (0) 20 7386 0927
Fax: +44 (0) 20 7386 7436
www.phillipalepley.com
Designer bridalwear

Sarah Owen
www.sarahowenlondon.co.uk
Designer bridalwear

Caroline Parkes
2nd Floor, 4 Morie Street
London
SW18 1SL
Tel: +44 (0) 20 8875 9669
www.carolineparkes.com
Designer bridalwear

Stewart Parvin
14 Motcomb Street
London
SW1X 8LB
Tel: +44 (0) 20 7235 1125
shirenefulton@stewartparvin.com
www.stewartparvin.com
Designer bridalwear

Antonia Pugh-Thomas
671a Fulham Road
London
SW6 5PZ
Tel: +44 (0) 20 7731 7582
Fax: +44 (0) 20 7384 3907
www.antoniapugh-thomas.co.uk
Designer bridalwear

Sesay
203A Belsize Road
London
NW6 4AA
Tel: +44 (0) 20 7328 2822
Bridalwear

Maggie Sottero
www.maggiesottero.com
Bridalwear
Stores worldwide

Elizabeth Todd Designs
3 Chiltern Street
London
W1U 7PB
Tel: +44 (0) 20 7224 2773
www.elizabethtodd.com
Designer bridalwear

Robinson Valentine
4 Hornton Place
London
W8 4LZ
Tel: +44 (0) 20 7937 3839
Fax: +44 (0) 20 7937 4572
www.robinsonvalentine.com
Designer bridalwear

Vera Wang
Flagship Salon
991 Madison Avenue
New York, NY 10021
Tel: +001 212 628 3400
www.verawang.com
Bridalwear, ready-to-wear,
footwear, jewelry, fragrance
Outlets worldwide,
also sold through:
The Wedding Shop
171 Fulham Road
London
SW3 6JW
Tel: +44 (0) 20 7838 0171

ACKNOWLEDGEMENTS

Chrysalis Books Group Plc is committed to respecting the intellectual property rights of others. We have therefore taken all reasonable efforts to ensure that the reproduction of all content on these pages is done with the full consent of copyright owners. If you are aware of any unintentional omissions please contact the company directly so that any necessary corrections may be made for future editions.

1 ©Robin Lowe-Abstract Creative; 2 SaraSusa/Virgin Bride; 6 James Gilberd/ Photospace; 7 Collection of Sarah Hunnings; 8 ©Amanda Lockhart; 9 Collection of Ian & Betty Gillan; 10 Collection of Amanda Saborn Hutt; 11 Collection of Antonia Pugh-Thomas; 16 ©SNAP/Rex Features; 17TL ©Bettman/CORBIS; 17TR ©Sipa Press/Rex Features; 17B ©Quadrillion/CORBIS; 18 ©Tony McGee Photography/ www.tonymcgee.co.uk; 18/19, 20TL, 20TR, 20BL, 20BR, 21, 22T ©Robin Lowe-Abstract Creative; 22B Collection of Elizabeth Todd Designs; 23, 24, 25TL, 25TR, 25BL, 25BR ©Robin Lowe-Abstract Creative; 26/27 ©Hulton Archive/Getty Images; 27T, 27C ©Robin Lowe-Abstract Creative; 28T ©Tony McGee Photography/ www.tonymcgee.co.uk; 28B ©Robin Lowe-Abstract Creative; 29T ©SaraSusa/Virgin Bride; 29BL ©Robin Lowe-Abstract Creative; 29BR ©SaraSusa/Virgin Bride; 30, 31 ©Robin Lowe-Abstract Creative; 36 ©Hulton Archive/Getty Images; 37L ©Simon/Ferreira/Rex Features; 37R ©SaraSusa/Virgin Bride; 38/39, 40T ©Robin Lowe-Abstract Creative; 40B Collection of Caroline Parkes; 41 Collection of Laura Wilson; 42, 43 ©Robin Lowe-Abstract Creative; 44 Collection of Caroline Parkes; 45, 46, 47TL, 47TR; ©Robin Lowe-Abstract Creative; 47BR Collection of Caroline Parkes, 47BR Collection of Stewart Parvin; 48, 49T, 49B ©Robin Lowe-Abstract Creative; 50 Collection of Caroline Parkes; 51 ©Robin Lowe-Abstract Creative; 56 ©Stewart Turkington/Rex Features; 57T ©David Hartley/Rex Features; 57B ©Albert Ferreira/Rex Features; 58 Collection of Lois Oldfield; 59 ©Hulton Archive/Getty Images; 60, 61, 62 ©Robin Lowe-Abstract Creative; 63 Collection of Caroline Parkes; 64, 65 ©Robin Lowe-Abstract Creative; 66 ©Tony McGee Photography/www.tonymcgee.co.uk; 67 Collection of Sarah Owen London; 72/73 ©Tim Graham/Getty Images; 73T ©Getty Images; 73B ©Charbonneau/BEI/Rex Features;74T ©Charlotte Rushton; 74B Collection of Antonia Pugh-Thomas; 75, 76, 77, 78L ©Robin Lowe-Abstract Creative; 78R Collection of Stewart Parvin; 79, 80 ©Robin Lowe-Abstract Creative; 81 Collection of Sarah Hunnings; 82, 83T, 83B ©Robin Lowe-Abstract Creative; 84 Collection of Stewart Parvin; 85 ©Robin Lowe-Abstract Creative; 86/87 ©James Gilberd/Photospace; 88 ©Getty Images; 89 ©Robin Lowe-Abstract Creative; 90 Gilles Piel/Image Décisive/Patricia Hopkins; 91 ©Marie-Line Denis, 2004; 96T ©Bettman/CORBIS; 96B ©Reuters/CORBIS; 97 ©rien/CORBIS SYGMA; 98TL, 98TR, 98BL, 98BR ©Robin Lowe-Abstract Creative; 99 Collection of Caroline Parkes; 100 ©Robin Lowe-Abstract Creative; 101TL ©Tom Bader/www.tombaderphotography.com; 101TR Collection of Emily Preece-Morrison; 101B ©Studio Images UK/www.studioimages.co.uk; 102, 103T, 103C, 103B, 104/5, 105, 106TL ©Robin Lowe-Abstract Creative; 106TR Collection of Caroline Parkes; 106CL ©Martin Rice/ Collection of Antonia Pugh-Thomas; 106CR Collection of Caroline Parkes; 106BL, 106BR ©Robin Lowe-Abstract Creative; 107 Collection of Sarah Owen London; 112 ©Hulton Archive/Getty Images;

First published in Great Britain in 2005 by
PAVILION BOOKS

An imprint of **Chrysalis** Books Group plc

The Chrysalis Building
Bramley Road
London W10 6SP
www.chrysalisbooks.co.uk

COMMISSIONING EDITOR: Kate Oldfield
SENIOR EDITOR: Emily Preece-Morrison
DESIGNER: Isobel Gillan
ILLUSTRATOR: Camilla Dixon
PICTURE RESEARCH: Sarah Stewart-Richardson

ISBN 1 86205 702 8

A CIP catalogue record for this book is available from
the British Library.

10 9 8 7 6 5 4 3 2 1

Reproduction by ClassicScan Pte Ltd, Singapore
Printed and bound by Imago printers, Thailand

This book can be ordered direct from the publisher.
Contact the marketing department, but try your bookshop first.